LIFE IN OUTER SPACE

The Search for Extraterrestrials

Kim McDonald

RAINTREE
STECK-VAUGHN
PUBLISHERS

A Harcourt Company

Austin · New York
www.steck-vaughn.com

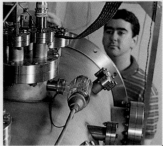

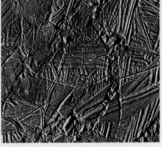

For Rachel

Steck-Vaughn Company

First published 2001 by Raintree Steck-Vaughn Publishers,
an imprint of Steck-Vaughn Company.

Copyright © 2001 Turnstone Publishing Group, Inc.
Copyright © 2001, text, by Kim McDonald

Library of Congress Cataloging-in-Publication Data

McDonald, Kim
    Life in outer space / Kim McDonald.
        p. cm. — (Turnstone space explorer book)
    Includes bibliographic references and index.
    ISBN 0-7398-2213-6 (hardcover)   ISBN 0-7398-2223-3 (softcover)
      1. — Life on other planets — Juvenile literature. [1. Life on other planets.] I. Title.
  II. Series.
  QB54.M526 2000   00-031075
  576.8'39—dc21

For information about this and other Turnstone reference books and educational materials,
visit Turnstone Publishing Group on the World Wide Web at http://www.turnstonepub.com.

Photo and illustration credits listed on page 64 constitute part of this copyright page.

Printed and bound in the United States of America

1 2 3 4 5 6 7 8 9 0 LB 05 04 03 02 01 00

Contents

1
WHAT IS ASTROBIOLOGY?

"What we really want to find—let's face it—is an Earthlike planet. . . . It would be fantastic if that happened in our lifetime, but the life we find may be only algae. Life may be close to us in space, but not in time."—Alan Boss

What is life? And where do you find it? These are two easy questions, you might say. Of course, everyone knows the difference between a Labrador retriever and a clump of dirt. And finding worms, weeds, and other living things in your backyard isn't hard, either. But ask those two questions about life elsewhere in the universe and the questions become much harder to answer. Do all living things look like the animals and plants on Earth? Can they live without oxygen to breathe or water to drink? Where are we likely to find other life?

Finding the answers to those questions is part of the goal of astrobiology. Astrobiology is a new area of science. It concentrates on the search for life beyond Earth. Astrobiologists look for any kind of living things. They may be as small as tiny bacteria, a form of life made of only one cell. Or they may be much larger than we are.

Most scientists in this search aren't biologists. And they don't usually call themselves astrobiologists. They are scientists from different fields. But they are all trying to understand how life evolved, or changed, on Earth and elsewhere.

(above)
The picture above shows something living, a painted lizard. It sits on something nonliving, a rock. What defines living? With new discoveries, the answer continues to grow larger.

(left)
Sometimes, even on Earth, it is difficult to determine if something is alive. The universe is a big place. Will scientists be able to recognize life in other places?

5

Is It Alive?

Earth is full of life—in the water, on the land, and in the air. But what defines life? On Earth, these are the basics:

- Able to repair and maintain itself—
This plant can replace a lost leaf.

- Able to grow—
Plants like this one grow from seeds.

- Able to reproduce—
This plant reproduces through pollination.

- Able to take and use energy and materials from surroundings—
This plant uses water, carbon dioxide, and sunlight.

- Made of organic matter—
All life on Earth is made of organic, or carbon-containing, material.

- Will die—
All life on Earth dies, including this plant.

That's fine for Earth, but what about space? What do scientists look for as signs of extraterrestrial life? They use the same characteristics as for life on Earth. For example, scientists may look for the presence of carbon in meteorites from other planets.

Some scientists search for planets around stars other than our sun. Others brave the cold of Antarctica to hunt for rocks from space. Or they travel miles beneath Earth's surface to look for bacteria that don't need oxygen or sunlight to live. Some hunt in our galaxy for water and the chemicals that are necessary for life as we know it. And still others look for signals coming from extraterrestrial, or non-Earth, civilizations.

Receiving signals from intelligent life like ourselves may be unlikely. Some scientists think the life they will first find may be very small, like bacteria. Bacteria exist in great numbers. They can exist in places where most other living things can't.

Looking for Signs

But what if life in space isn't like bacteria? What if it isn't like anything scientists have ever seen? How will scientists know if what they find is living? Biologists define life as the activities necessary for living things. These activities include growth, movement, and reproduction.

It's hard to tell if something billions of miles away is growing, moving, and reproducing. The activities of living things on Earth produce some effects, however, that can be seen from far away. One effect is the addition of oxygen to the atmosphere, the blanket of gas that surrounds planets and stars. Oxygen is released by plants when they change sunlight and materials into energy.

Answering Questions

Does all life need oxygen? Some ocean animals, like these tubeworms, use hydrogen sulfide instead. This discovery opened up new questions for scientists about what's necessary for life.

To answer these kinds of questions, NASA (the National Aeronautics and Space Administration) started the Astrobiology Institute. The institute is made up of research centers and universities throughout the world.

Institute scientists want to understand how life began on Earth and how it continues to exist and change. Knowing this may help in the search for life on other planets.

Planet Finder

Sometime between 2010 and 2020, NASA plans to launch a group of telescopes into space. These telescopes will take pictures of planets around distant stars.

This group of telescopes, called the Terrestrial Planet Finder, is shown below in an artist's drawing. Together these telescopes will help bring planets around nearby stars into focus. During its six-year mission, the Terrestrial Planet Finder will search for planets around 1,000 bright stars that are near the sun. One of the stars it will take a closer look at is Proxima Centauri, shown in the picture to the right. Proxima Centauri is the star nearest the sun.

Astrobiologists look for this sign of life. This search is difficult because many of the places where scientists are looking for life are very far from Earth.

What is another sign of extraterrestrial life? Life's raw materials are a good sign. On Earth, the raw materials that form living things include carbon, hydrogen, oxygen, and nitrogen. Water, a combination of hydrogen and oxygen, is one of the first things scientists look for because it is so important to life on Earth. Water is a major part of living things. Human beings are about 60 percent water.

Scientists also need to know the conditions necessary for life. How warm or cold can a planet be and still have life? People on Earth live in a small range of temperatures. In this range, water can stay liquid. For the most part, the other planets in our solar system are either too hot or too cold to hold liquid water.

It is unlikely that life exists in such harsh climates, but is it possible? Astrobiologists doubt it. But to be sure, they study the coldest and the hottest places on Earth for signs of life. If life exists in extreme environments on Earth, maybe it exists in space.

Scientists believe water once flowed on the surface of Mars. They also think that liquid water probably exists below the surface of Europa, one of Jupiter's moons. But how common is water on planets? Once they know the answer to this question, astrobiologists will have a better idea of the number of places where life could exist.

In our solar system, Mars and Europa may offer the best possibilities for life. But many astrobiologists think that a better place to look for extraterrestrial life is outside our solar system. With more than 200 billion stars in our galaxy, there are a lot of places to look.

Astronomers are scientists who study objects in outer space. They have already found more than three times as many planets outside our solar system than in it. And their telescope searches are turning up more planets every few months. Someday, astronomers hope to find planets where life exists.

Water, Water Everywhere

Astronomers have found water in many places in outer space. Is this water the source of Earth's oceans? Could the water on Mars and Europa have come from somewhere else in space? Some scientists think so, but even they aren't sure how it happened.

It is possible that some of the water in space may freeze on grains of dust. The grains slowly grow larger. In time these dirty snowballs may become comets. Maybe the comets brought a lot of water when they struck Earth early in its history.

This image of Europa was taken by NASA's Galileo spacecraft. The patterns in the close-up of Europa's surface may have been made by ice.

Planet Goldilocks

What would a planet with life look like? Scientists think it might be the kind of planet that Goldilocks would choose. The planet wouldn't be too big. But it wouldn't be too small, either. If it was too small, it couldn't hold an atmosphere. And it wouldn't be too hot or too cold, so there could be liquid water. To be the right temperature, a planet needs to be the right distance from its sun or have another source of heat.

Astronomer Dimitar Sasselov developed detailed models that he believes represent the way stars and planetary systems form and change. From these models Dimitar concludes that there might be many more places where life could exist than scientists first thought.

In our solar system, Earth is the only planet where life is known to exist. Life might form on a planet's moon, too, if the conditions are right. One of Jupiter's moons, Europa, might have the right conditions to support life under its surface.

Mercury is the closest planet to the sun. Its surface is too hot to allow liquid water.

Earth is just right. Its surface temperatures allow liquid water.

Mars has possibilities of life, too. The Mars surface temperatures could allow liquid water. But no water has yet been found.

The surface of Venus is even hotter than Mercury's, so there is no liquid water on Venus.

Scientists believe that life on Jupiter, Saturn, Uranus, and Neptune is very unlikely. But they cannot yet rule out this possibility.

Pluto's surface has the coldest temperatures of any planet in our solar system. Scientists believe life is even less likely to exist on Pluto.

Note that this picture groups the planets of our solar system together so that they can be compared to one another. The planets in this picture were not drawn to scale. The angle of their tilts and the distances between them are also incorrect.

HOW DO WE FIND PLANETS?

"The technology needed to find Earthlike planets...is about a decade away."—David Charbonneau

Before scientists find life existing on planets outside our solar system, they must first try to find these planets. This kind of search began in the 1950s. The search can be difficult because these planets are often very hard to detect.

From Earth, it is easy to find Mars, Venus, or Jupiter in the night sky. These planets reflect sunlight like a road reflects light from a car's headlights. But it would be hard to see those planets if they were hundreds of trillions of miles away and hidden by the bright light from a star. So astronomers search for distant planets in other ways.

On a stormy evening in March 1988, astronomer David Latham turned his telescope toward a star in the constellation Coma Berenices. The star he was studying, HD 114762, is thought to be like our sun. The star seemed ordinary to Dave, except for one thing. It seemed to change its motion toward or away from Earth periodically, or at regular intervals. Dave, who works at the Harvard-Smithsonian Center for Astrophysics (the CfA), was puzzled. Why did the star move?

A planet might be the answer. When a planet orbits, or travels around, a star, the star also orbits the planet.

(above)
Jupiter is the largest planet in our solar system. It is also one of the brightest objects in the nighttime sky. This is how Jupiter looks using a backyard telescope. The image was made using a 20-centimeter (8-inch) optical telescope in Malden, Massachusetts.

(left)
Dave Latham is shown standing beside a Harvard-Smithsonian telescope he often works with to make his observations.

13

The Wave Model of Light

Astronomers use models to study the stars, including models of how light behaves. Models are useful in predicting light's behavior. Light is very mysterious. The more scientists study it, the more mysterious it seems. But some of its properties, or characteristics, can be modeled fairly easily.

In one model, it is assumed that light moves in waves. Each wave has a top and a bottom, or a crest and a trough. A wavelength is the distance between two crests or the distance between two troughs. Wavelengths of light can be from near zero to near infinity.

Waves travel one after another, like the cars of a train. It is possible to measure the frequency of waves, or the number of crests or troughs, that pass a certain point in a certain amount of time. A wave's frequency multiplied by its length equals its speed. All light waves travel at the same speed. Each wavelength of light has its own frequency. And each frequency has its own wavelength. It is their wavelengths (or frequencies) that make light waves different.

The light we see is called the visible spectrum. Light in the visible spectrum has a certain range of wavelengths. In a rainbow, different wavelengths of light separate. They appear in this order—red, orange, yellow, green, blue, indigo, and violet. In the wave model, wavelengths of light become shorter in this same order. Red light has the longest wavelengths, and violet has the shortest wavelengths.

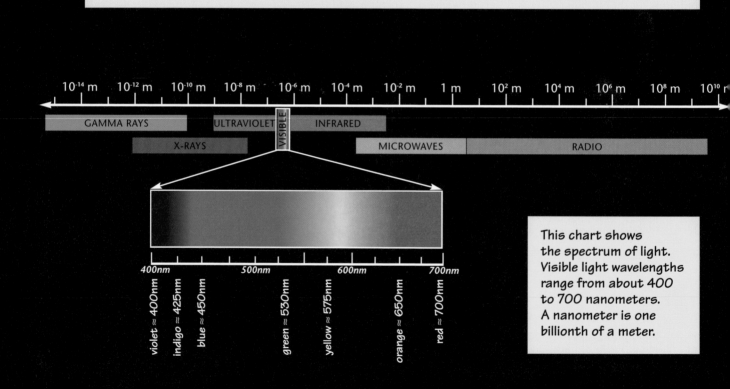

This chart shows the spectrum of light. Visible light wavelengths range from about 400 to 700 nanometers. A nanometer is one billionth of a meter.

The chart above shows the names used for light of different wavelengths. Light with the shortest wavelengths is called gamma rays. Light with the longest wavelengths is called radio waves.

The star and planet are a system, or group of objects that affect each other. Both the star and the planet go around an imaginary point within the system. This point is called the center of mass. It represents the average position of the system's mass. It is much closer to the star because the star is more massive. As the star goes around the center of mass point, its distance from Earth periodically changes. The motion of the star in the direction of Earth also changes periodically. This motion can sometimes be measured from Earth if the motion itself is not too small.

Could an orbiting planet cause the star HD 114762 to move periodically? But if it were a planet, Dave thought, it would have to be much more massive than Jupiter. Otherwise, the planet could not affect the star's orbit enough for Dave's equipment to detect the change. Also, the planet would have to be close to the star.

The closer a planet is to a star, the shorter its year is. A planet's year is the time it takes to orbit a star completely. If there were a planet orbiting star HD 114762, the planet's year would be only 84 days long! It would be much closer to the star than Earth is to our sun. When Dave first made his observations in 1988, most astronomers thought such a small orbit for such a large planet was impossible.

HD 114762, shown above, is about 130 light-years from Earth. A light-year is the distance light travels in one year. The body orbiting the star has at least nine times the mass of the planet Jupiter.

Here is the instrument that Dave uses to measure the periodic movement of stars toward or away from Earth. It is a spectrograph, an instrument that separates light into its colors. It is attached behind the 1.5-meter (61-inch) diameter mirror of the Wyeth reflector telescope.

Viewing system
This television camera makes an image on a TV monitor. The image shows the astronomer where the telescope is pointing.

Spectrograph
Starlight enters the telescope and passes through the spectrograph. The spectrograph then separates the light into its colors, that is, into a spectrum.

Detector
The detector, along with other electronic devices, allows a computer to record the spectrum. The computer record can then be analyzed, or studied.

Star Speedometer

After Dave made his observations, he checked and rechecked his data, or information. He soon became convinced that there wasn't any problem with his equipment or his experiment. He felt certain that a massive planet or some other massive object was causing the star to move.

How did Dave know? With help from his detector and other electronic devices, Dave collected spectra of the light given off by HD 114762. When he compared the spectra collected almost every night in a long series of observations, he found evidence of periodic changes in the star's light. The changes had a pattern. The light appeared bluer, then redder, then bluer again, and so on.

This pattern of behavior fits a model called the Doppler effect. A star's color observed on Earth depends on the direction in which the star is moving. When a star moves away from Earth, its light appears redder. As a star moves toward Earth, its light appears bluer. This color change works like a kind of stellar, or star, speedometer. The color change can show astronomers how fast a star moves toward or away from Earth.

This method of determining star speed was not new in 1988. But instruments available at that time could not measure changes in speed less than about 400 meters (about 1,300 feet) per second. Dave's spectrograph, for example, could not have detected the changes in our sun's movement caused by Jupiter and Saturn. That change is never more than about 13 meters (about 43 feet) per second. But if a planet were many times more massive than Jupiter and much closer to its parent star than Jupiter is to the sun, the star might move fast enough to measure with a stellar speedometer.

That's what Dave hoped when he turned his telescope toward HD 114762. From his measurements of the periodic changes in the star's speed toward or away from

The Wyeth reflector telescope Dave uses is housed here at the Oak Ridge Observatory in Harvard, Massachusetts. Scientists use it to study the movement of stars, comets, and asteroids.

Didier Queloz (left) and Michel Mayor are standing in front of the Euler 1.2-meter (nearly 4-foot) diameter Swiss telescope at the La Silla Observatory in Elqui, Chile.

Earth, he decided that a planet was orbiting the star. Some astronomers consider Dave's work the first discovery of a planet orbiting a star outside our solar system. Others think the object may be too massive to be a planet. Astronomers are still unable to determine the mass of the object Dave discovered.

More Discoveries

In 1995 Swiss astronomers Didier Queloz and Michel Mayor used a stellar speedometer to find the first clear example of a planet orbiting a star like our sun. The planet appeared likely to be far less massive than the object Dave found, so there was less debate about whether to call it a planet. It probably had a mass nearly as large as Jupiter's. But the astronomers were shocked by another characteristic. The planet's year was only four days long. The astronomers used this four-day year to calculate the planet's distance from its star. It is much closer to its star than Mercury is to our sun. "Because the planet is orbiting so close to its star, the planet's surface must be much too hot to hold life," explains Robert "Bob" Noyes. He is a CfA astronomer who helped confirm the discovery.

Two years later, Bob and a team of scientists discovered another Jupiter-sized planet. This planet orbits the star Rho Coronae Borealis. Since then, more Jupiter-sized planets and perhaps smaller, Saturn-sized planets have been found around other stars. Many planets were first discovered by Geoffrey Marcy, of the University of California at Berkeley, and Paul Butler, of the Carnegie Institution in Washington, D. C.

The recently discovered planets are much larger than most or perhaps all of the planets in our solar system. Also, most of the orbits of these planets are much smaller than the orbits of the planets in our solar system. As technology improves, astronomers may be able to detect solar systems more like ours.

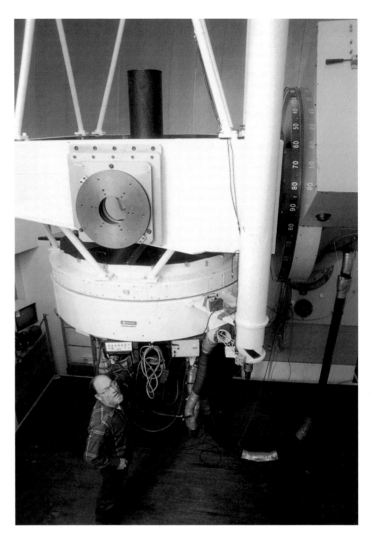

Astronomer Bob Noyes is standing in front of a spectrometer mounted on a 1.5-meter (61-inch) telescope at the Whipple Observatory near Tucson, Arizona. Bob is part of a team that uses the spectrometer to detect a star's periodic movement toward or away from Earth.

In April 1999 two teams of scientists announced a discovery of a solar system with three planets. Bob's team at the CfA and Geoffrey's team at Berkeley worked separately at different observatories. The teams used different kinds of speedometers, but they reached the same conclusion. This made their results more convincing.

Both teams observed the periodic movements of the star Upsilon Andromedae. To explain the movements they saw, the teams determined that there must be three massive planets orbiting the star. Measurements tell them that the outermost planet has a mass about four times greater than the mass of Jupiter. It orbits the star once every 3.5 years. The middle planet is about twice as massive as Jupiter. It orbits once every 242 days. And the innermost planet is about three-fourths as massive as Jupiter. It whizzes around the star every 4.6 days. The planets are much closer to the star than Jupiter is to the sun. It takes Jupiter nearly 12 years to orbit the sun. The discovery of three planets orbiting one star showed that there may be many other solar systems with more than one planet.

In June 1999 Dave Latham, working with a team of Israeli and Swiss astronomers, detected a periodic movement in another star. This motion was the result of a rapidly orbiting planet. David Charbonneau was assigned to observe the star closely. He looked for any dimming of the star's light as the planet passed between Earth and the star. If he was successful, astronomers would be directly detecting a planet outside our solar system for the first time!

David Charbonneau was one of the two astronomers who first observed the dimming of star HD 209458.

Then, in August and September of that year, David and Tim Brown, an astronomer in Colorado, found the evidence they needed. They saw the planet eclipse, or block out, some of the star's light as it passed in front of star HD 209458. They watched two eclipses from beginning to end. Greg Henry of Tennessee State University, who was part of another team headed by Geoffrey Marcy and Paul Butler, saw part of another eclipse a few months later.

This discovery convinced scientists that they were really seeing planets. "We're beginning to see just the tip of the iceberg," says Bob. "We're seeing the stars that are easy to see, the ones with the close-in planets."

This is an artist's picture of star HD 209458 and its planet. In the picture, the planet is passing in front of the star, causing the star's light to dim. It takes about two hours for the planet to travel all the way across the star when viewed from Earth.

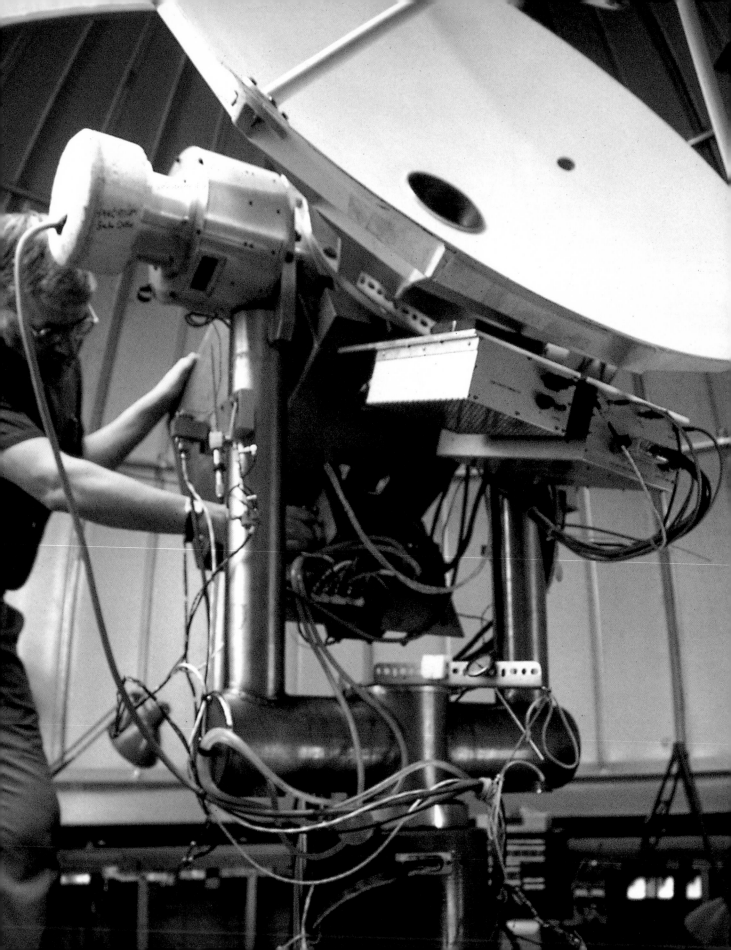

LIFE'S RAW MATERIALS

"I used to say that [our time could be compared to] the age of Newton, but now I have to say to my students that now is by far the best, most fruitful period of all."—Patrick Thaddeus

Patrick Thaddeus sat down in front of his computer in Cambridge, Massachusetts. On the roof of the building where Pat worked, his telescope scanned the sky. Most astronomers work at night on the tops of mountains.

But Pat, an astronomer at the CfA, can work in broad daylight in the middle of a city. That's because he isn't using an optical telescope; he's using a radio telescope. Pat isn't looking for distant stars or planets, but for the chemicals needed to produce life.

Radio telescopes can sometimes be bigger than a ten-story building. They are often devoted to collecting radio waves given off by distant galaxies. But Pat's telescope is called the mini. The biggest part of his telescope is a satellite dish that collects radio-frequency waves given off by objects in space. The mini can easily fit on the roof of most buildings.

The mini's small size gives it a larger field of view. It can see more of the sky at one time than a larger telescope. So Pat can collect radio waves from big things.

(above)
The first mini was built by Pat Thaddeus and fellow scientists at Columbia University in New York City in the early 1970s. A "twin" of the mini is now in place in Cerro Tololo, Chile. It scans the sky above Earth's Southern Hemisphere.

(left)
The original mini, now at the CfA, is used by scientists to measure radio waves given off by carbon monoxide molecules in space.

23

The photo above shows the constellation Orion as it appears in the night sky. It has been outlined so it stands out.

He's looking for giant clouds of gas and dust. Pat and other astrobiologists think that some of the materials needed for life may be in these clouds. Pat looks inside the clouds for molecules that contain carbon. These are called organic molecules because every living thing on Earth is made of them.

Water and organic molecules had to be on Earth for life to begin. Where did they come from? Astronomers have discovered that both types of molecules are present in the Milky Way galaxy. How were they made?

The molecules are present in dark patches in the sky. These patches are dark because they block the light from stars behind them. The patches are really clouds of gas and dust. They are called molecular clouds, because they are full of molecules.

Hunting for Dark Clouds

Pat and fellow CfA astronomer Tom Dame hunt for these clouds with their radio telescope. They find them by looking for something that's in the clouds. They look for carbon monoxide, the same molecule that is in car exhaust. Carbon monoxide molecules give off radio waves of a particular wavelength, or frequency.

To detect radio waves given off by carbon monoxide molecules in a cloud, Pat and Tom attach a device called a spectrometer to the radio telescope. A spectrometer is like a spectrograph, the device used by Dave.

To detect radio waves, Pat and Tom tune the spectrometer more precisely to a particular range of wavelengths or frequencies. Frequencies of light given off by a molecule can identify the molecule, just as a fingerprint identifies a specific person. Pat and Tom can

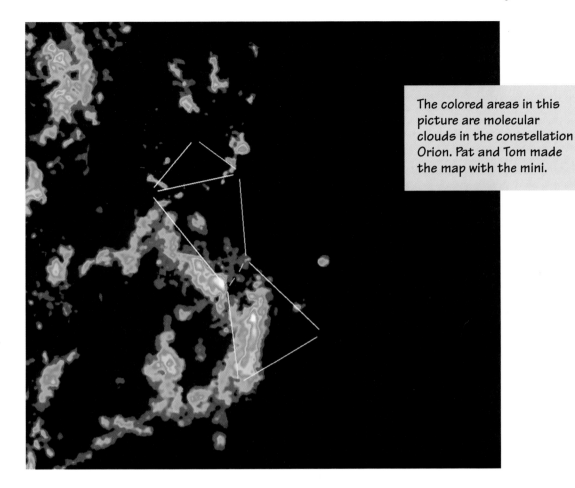

The colored areas in this picture are molecular clouds in the constellation Orion. Pat and Tom made the map with the mini.

identify carbon monoxide molecules by one of the frequencies of light these molecules give off.

The radio frequencies Pat and Tom look for aren't close to the frequencies of radio, television, or most other electronic signals produced by humans. They are much higher. Pat and Tom use their computer to tune the spectrometer to one of the frequencies (or wavelengths) that distinguish the radio waves given off by carbon monoxide. Then, Pat and Tom search the sky. The telescope's computer lets them know when the telescope is pointing in a direction from which radio waves of this frequency are coming. When the waves are found, Pat and Tom know they have found a place that will probably have molecular clouds.

How to Map a Galaxy with a Radio Telescope

This map shows molecular clouds in half of the Milky Way. These clouds are believed to be made mostly of hydrogen and helium. These gases are hard to detect. Astronomers locate molecular clouds by detecting radio waves from the carbon monoxide in the clouds.

2

The spectrometer shown above on the right analyzes, or studies, the radio waves picked up by the mini.

3

A computer makes a graph of the relative strengths of the light received at various frequencies. Astronomers know when they have detected a molecular cloud because they see a peak in the graph at the frequency of carbon monoxide. If there is a lot of carbon monoxide detected, there is a cloud in that particular direction in the sky.

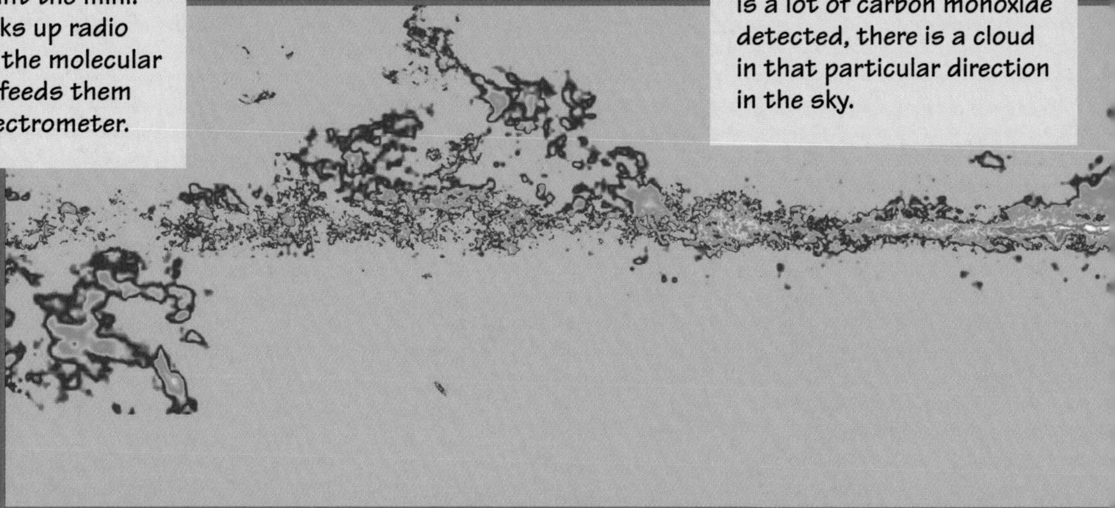

1

To map molecular clouds, the astronomers begin by choosing a direction in which to point the mini. The mini picks up radio waves from the molecular clouds and feeds them into the spectrometer.

This is a picture of a spiral galaxy that is like our galaxy, the Milky Way. We can't take a picture like this one of the Milky Way because we are inside it. If this were the Milky Way, Earth would be located on one of the spiral arms. A galaxy swirls like water going down a drain. The clouds closer to the center move faster.

Center of Galaxy

4

Each time astronomers detect molecular clouds in a particular direction, they add one point to their map. This map is made from about one-half million points. The colors represent the relative strengths of the light given off by carbon monoxide. The colors range from dark blue (weakest) to white (strongest).

Spiral Arm

Making a Molecular Cloud

Scientists already know the frequencies of the radio waves given off by many molecules. But how does Pat hunt for unknown ones? Many molecules found in space are not found naturally on Earth. To find out the frequencies of the radio waves given off by these molecules, Pat makes new molecules in his lab. He makes a small molecular cloud and measures the frequencies given off by its molecules.

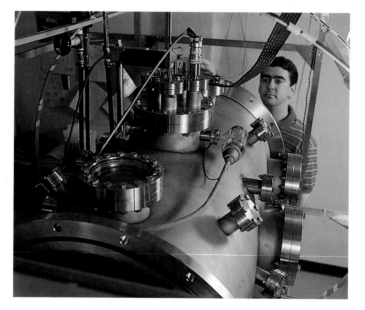

Here astronomer Michael McCarthy conducts an experiment. Michael is making a miniature molecular cloud in a chamber in Pat Thaddeus' lab. Michael is closing the side door of the chamber after adjusting the equipment.

To make a miniature cloud, Pat shoots a mixture of gases into a chamber that is one meter (about three feet) long. The chamber has been almost completely emptied of air. While the gas enters the tube, Pat sets off a 1,000-volt spark of electricity.

In less than one second, the electrical spark produces new molecules in the gas. It happens as the gas moves at a very high speed from one end of the chamber to the other. "We know from experience that you can make these things," Pat says. But no one really knows how the new molecules form.

The scientists then identify any new molecules that form by the frequencies of the radio waves they give off. Using this process, Pat and his co-workers have recently found 51 new molecules. Seven of those molecules have already been found in space.

On Earth big molecules tend to branch somewhat like trees. In space many big molecules are long, straight chains. The biggest molecule that Pat and his CfA co-workers had detected by June 1999 was a straight chain whose backbone is made from carbon with hydrogen and some nitrogen atoms attached.

But there are similarities between molecules found in

space and those on Earth. So far most of the 125 molecules found in space are organic molecules. At least some of the chemical reactions that are needed for life on Earth must therefore take place elsewhere in space. Chemical reactions are changes in the groupings of atoms in molecules.

Pat and Tom think it may not be long before more of the materials needed for life are found in space. Only a tiny fraction of the Milky Way galaxy has been searched for big molecules. "If you compare the whole area of the [Milky Way] galaxy to the size of Washington, D.C., the area that has been surveyed is about the size of a dinner plate," says Pat. "We just don't know much about how many big molecules exist or where they are."

Pat and Tom have put together the most complete map ever produced of the galaxy's molecular clouds. The map shows many molecular clouds that are millions of trillions of kilometers wide. Because molecular clouds are so common in space and so large, they are good signs for scientists who search for extraterrestrial life.

Pat uses this chamber to make molecular clouds in his laboratory. He makes molecules that may exist in space, but not on Earth. Then, he measures the frequencies that they give off. In this way, he knows which frequencies to hunt for in space.

Observation windows

Adjustable mirror

Fixed mirror

Gas enters through tubes in the side door.

The pump forces out the gas after the experiment.

ROCKS FROM OUTER SPACE

"Wait until you see this thing."— Roberta Score

As a child Ralph Harvey dreamed of being an astronaut. But not the kind of astronaut he saw walking on the moon. "I wanted to be more the Buck Rogers kind of astronaut," he remembers, "with my own little space buggy. I wanted to fight nasty aliens on some planet where the milk is blue and plants are red."

Ralph is a geologist from Case Western Reserve University in Cleveland, Ohio. Traveling across the blue ice fields of East Antarctica in his red-and-white snowmobile, Ralph can see only ice and blowing snow in every direction. He may not be fighting aliens in outer space, but he is close to living his dream.

This place at the bottom of the world could easily pass for an alien planet. Rubber-soled "moon boots" keep the scientists from slipping on the ice. A kind of hockey mask protects their faces from the wind. The boots and masks make them look like astronauts.

The team is in Antarctica to collect meteorites, chunks of rock from outer space that have crashed on Earth. Meteorites are important to planetary geologists, scientists who study the material of which planets are made. Some meteorites are pieces of rocks that have come from other planets. Scientists think that these meteorites may be the result of an orbiting object, like an asteroid, that struck Earth.

(above)
Although no people officially call Antarctica "home," there are many scientific research projects underway there. At times, thousands of people are working on this mostly frozen continent.

(left)
One of the best ways to get around is by snowmobile, not dogsled. Dogs are not allowed in Antarctica, to protect the native seal population from diseases dogs may carry.

Here's the base camp in "Meteorite City." The camp is where Ralph's team stays while they hunt for meteorites. In this picture, they are still stowing gear, but one tent has been set up. The Antarctic wind makes that hard work.

The rocks often hold organic materials and sometimes even water. These are the same materials that are in molecular clouds. The materials in these rocks may have come from the molecular cloud that made our solar system more than 4 billion years ago.

Ralph is the leader of the expedition. He and Bill Cassidy, the scientist who started these searches, call them "the poor person's space probe." Space probes can cost hundreds of millions of dollars. But "for less than 100,000 dollars a year, we can bring back samples of another planet," says Ralph.

Rock Hunters

The meteorite hunts take place just once each year. They happen in November when it's summer in Antarctica. On this trip the scientists take a 14-hour flight from the United States to New Zealand. Then, they take another full-day flight to McMurdo Station, the main U.S. research base in Antarctica. From there, they fly on a twin-propeller plane that has skis instead of wheels for landing on the ice. This plane takes them directly to the East Antarctic ice sheet.

Many meteorites have fallen on Antarctica over time. They are covered by ice, but eventually the wind may uncover them. The scientists expect to find some of these meteorites on the ice sheet.

But why put up with the long trip and the cold weather? After all, geologists think the same number of meteorites falls on other places on Earth. There are three good reasons to look in Antarctica. Antarctic meteorites are better preserved and easier to spot against the snow. They are also left untouched. It is so cold in Antarctica that there are fewer bacteria. Bacteria can produce cavities, or holes, in meteorites just as they produce cavities in your teeth. The condition of a meteorite is important. A scientist must determine if the material in a meteorite came from space or got into the meteorite once it landed on Earth.

Because it's summer, the temperatures are warm for Antarctica. It's about -5.5°C (about 22°F). But sometimes, when the wind blows at 65 kilometers per hour (about 40 miles per hour), it can feel much, much colder. On very windy days the scientists usually stay in their tents. They can hunt meteorites anytime, day or night. The summer sun never sets in this part of Antarctica. It just makes a big circle in the sky. It's good for reading at three o'clock in the morning without a flashlight. But

Collecting on the Ice

Three-fifths of the 25,000 meteorites found on Earth have been collected in Antarctica. Meteorites also fall in other places. They are just easier to find on ice.

Over thousands of years, meteorites in Antarctica become trapped in ice. This ice moves outward about 10 to 20 meters (about 30 to 60 feet) per year. At the edges of the continent, the ice is pushed up, then worn away by wind. This erosion can cause meteorites that were buried by ice and snow to be uncovered.

Meet Nomad, the Meteorite Finder

Scientists cannot yet go to Mars to look for life, but maybe in the not-too-distant future, Nomad can go for them. This 730-kilogram (1,600-pound) robot, the size of a small car, looks for meteorites at Antarctica's McMurdo Station.

Nomad uses technology in place of human senses to search for meteorites. A high-resolution camera allows Nomad to look at the size, color, and shape of rocks as it approaches. Then, if a rock seems like a meteorite, Nomad uses a smaller camera to take a closer look. A special device allows the robot to determine what types of elements, or atoms, are present in the sample. A metal detector allows the robot to search for iron, an element common in many meteorites.

sleeping under the bright sun isn't always easy, especially when the wind pounds the sides of the tents like a jackhammer.

Six scientists live in three tents, two to a tent. Heat inside each tent comes from two small stoves. The scientists also use the stoves to heat meals and to melt ice for drinking. They turn the tent stoves off when they slip into their double-layered sleeping bags. Every morning the scientists wake up with a layer of ice on their pillows. The ice forms when the water vapor in their breath freezes.

The scientists drive around in their snowmobiles hoping to find chunks of another planet. But most of the meteorites they collect are bits of asteroids, small objects that revolve around the sun.

Most meteorites that reach Earth are only about the size of a thumb. But their black outer crust makes them easy to spot against the blue ice and white snow. On this trip the meteorite hunters pick up thumb-sized rocks. They also find some potato-sized rocks. These turn out to be the largest meteorites the scientists find on the trip. But they aren't the largest ever found in Antarctica. That prize goes to a meteorite found by scientist Bill Cassidy in 1976. It weighs 400 kilograms (about 900 pounds).

To prevent contamination, or getting non-meteorite material on the samples, the scientists use tongs to handle each meteorite they find. Each rock goes into a plastic bag that is free of Earth's bacteria and organic chemicals. This kind of bag is called a "clean bag."

While the meteorites are being collected, each one is measured, and the bag it goes into is labeled. Then, the bags of meteorites go into a protective box. At the end of

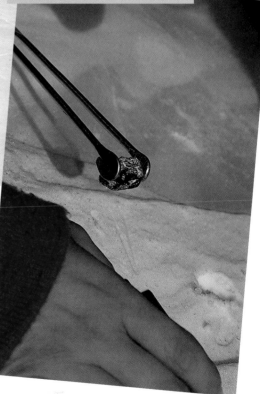

Here, Laurie Leshin of Arizona State University inspects a meteorite. Next, she carefully uses clean metal tongs to free it from the ice. No one touches any meteorite with their hands. That could contaminate the sample.

the collecting season, the box is flown to the Johnson Space Center in Houston, Texas. The box is kept cold so that the rocks are at the same temperature as they were on the ice. The scientists want to preserve any important evidence that might be in the samples.

At the Space Center, researchers will use special boxes with gloves attached to examine the meteorites. These glove boxes let researchers study the rocks without contaminating them.

Meteorites from Mars

On some of these expeditions, meteorite hunters have found strangely colored rocks. Some of these rocks have turned out to be pieces of the moon or Mars. For instance, in 1982 Ian Whillans of Ohio State University spotted the first lunar rock, or moon rock, ever found in Antarctica. "It looked different from any other lunar rock we had seen," recalls Ursula Marvin, a scientist at the CfA. "It was a complete surprise."

René Martinez, a scientist at the Institute for Lunar and Planetary Science in Houston, Texas, carefully slips a meteorite into a clean plastic bag. The bag will be taped shut and not opened again until it reaches the Johnson Space Center in Houston, Texas.

Following the discovery of a lunar rock in Antarctica, scientists found meteorites from even farther away—from another planet. Two days after Christmas in 1984, geologist Roberta "Robbie" Score of the Johnson Space Center was searching the ice for meteorites. She spotted an odd-looking rock. "It had a very green color," Robbie recalls. She couldn't stop thinking about the strange meteorite she'd collected. When it arrived at her laboratory, she told everyone, "Wait until you see this thing."

At the Johnson Space Center, the meteorite bags are opened in a clean, dust-free glove box. The samples are examined for signs of life, such as the presence of organic material.

But when the scientists unwrapped the meteorite, all they saw was a dull, grayish-green rock. "Everyone said, 'Yeah, Robbie, right.'"

The two-kilogram (about four-pound), potato-sized rock was labeled ALH84001. It sat on a shelf at the Space Center for nine years. But Robbie's first hunch about the meteorite proved correct. On a later hunt, researchers found a meteorite that looked just like ALH84001. It had tiny pockets of air that matched the atmosphere of Mars. Remembering Robbie's find, researchers tested that meteorite, as well. They concluded that it was from Mars, too.

Looking for Life

How did ALH84001 reach Earth? Scientists think it may have been thrown into space when a large asteroid or comet hit Mars about 16 million years ago. They think it may have drifted in space for millions of years before its path finally crossed Earth's path.

ALH84001 is the most important meteorite found so far because it's the oldest. It formed about 4.5 billion

(above)
The meteorite Robbie found, ALH84001, may have come from Mars.

(below)
This enlarged photograph of meteorite ALH84001 shows unusual tubelike structures. They are less than 1/1,000th the width of a human hair.

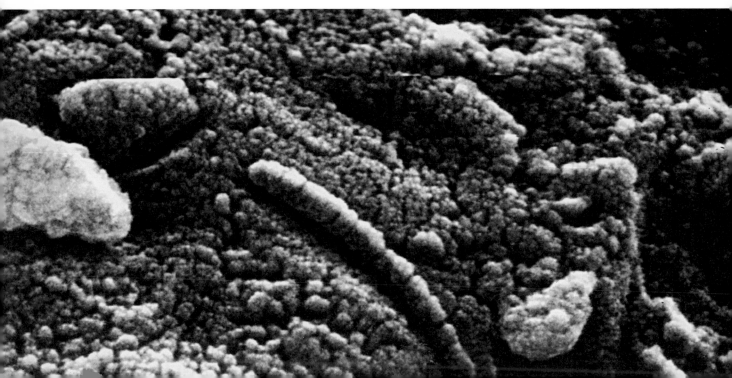

Robbie Score is one of many scientists who hope that life may exist on Mars. But most scientists doubt that life exists there.

years ago. Some of the materials inside the rock have been dated to 3.6 billion years ago. Scientists think that around that time, there may have been liquid water on Mars. Sometime later, water could have entered the rock through cracks in its surface. The water could have then deposited material inside.

Some scientists are excited about the material they found inside the meteorite because it is organic. This means that it is the type of material from which life can

Viking Landers

In 1976 two spacecraft, Viking 1 and Viking 2, landed on Mars. They took pictures of the Martian surface, and examined the planet's atmosphere and its surface. They also searched for evidence of life in the area near where they touched down. The spacecraft provided scientists with a very complete view of a small portion of Mars, but they failed to find any evidence of life. That's not surprising.

So far observations of Mars have not detected any water on the planet's surface and very little water in its atmosphere. But that may not always have been true. Evidence suggests that 3 to 4 billion years ago, rivers and lakes flowed on the Martian surface. If so, finding ancient fossils on Mars may not be out of the question.

be made. These scientists also found markings of what looked to them like the remains of microscopic bacteria. Some scientists think these bacteria were similar to bacteria that live in rocks far under Earth's surface. But others believe that the markings were not made by bacteria at all. They think these markings are most likely caused by natural mineral processes on Mars.

All together a dozen or so Martian meteorites have been identified. Each of these meteorites contains organic material. This material may have entered the meteorites after they reached Earth. But this material could also have been in the rock before the meteorites were ever thrown into space.

There is no proof that the meteorite found in Antarctica contains evidence of past Martian life. But the possibility has encouraged NASA to send probes to Mars. Perhaps the probes will answer the question of whether life ever existed on Mars. Something might even be living there now, deep under the Martian surface. That's why astrobiologists are so interested in finding out more about what's living deep inside Earth. It may help them know what to look for under the surface of Mars.

When scientists look at images of the surface of Mars, they see marks that may have been made by water. The lines in the small picture below may be paths once carved by flowing water.

These are possible water paths.

5

EXTREME BIOLOGY

"It's an eerie feeling, knowing you're that far down."—Jim Fredrickson

In November 1998 Jim Fredrickson put on coveralls and a miner's hat in preparation for the trip of his life. Jim is a microbiologist at the Pacific Northwest National Laboratory in Richland, Washington. He studies bacteria and other kinds of microorganisms, or tiny life forms. Microorganisms are too small to see without a microscope. The ones Jim studies live deep below Earth's surface. Most of the microorganisms he studies live in underground rocks and water in the United States. He finds them by using drills normally used to find oil.

On this November day, Jim was far from the United States. He was at the southern tip of Africa, near Johannesburg, one of South Africa's largest cities. He was about to go down into a working gold mine to try to find microorganisms living 3.2 kilometers (nearly 2 miles) below Earth's surface. Finding life deep beneath Earth's surface would be an important discovery for astrobiologists. If life can exist in such an extreme environment, maybe it can exist on other planets. Scientists would also have a reason to explore other remote places on Earth in their search for life. Equally important, the microorganisms might provide scientists with useful clues to how life could exist that far below the surface.

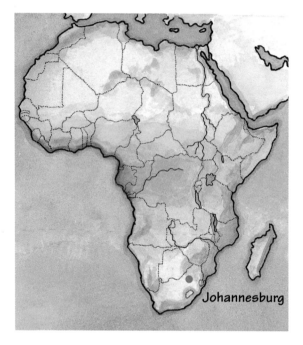

Johannesburg

(above)
South African gold mines, such as the one near Johannesburg, are sources of almost one-quarter of the world's gold. There may be other treasures in South Africa's deep mines, as well.

(left)
Geologist T. C. Onstott (right) talks with mine surveyor Raj Nair (left) while student Joost Hoek (center) looks on. The geologists are about to enter the East Driefontein mine, which is near Johannesburg, South Africa.

To reach the bottom of the mine, Jim and the other scientists entered a caged elevator. It took them down to a lower level. Then, they switched to another elevator. As they slowly went down, they could feel the heat of Earth's interior. It was about 50°C (about 120°F). Even worse than the heat was the humidity, or dampness, from pockets of heated underground water in the rock.

The humidity made the air thick with steam. Air had to be pumped from the surface into the tunnels so the scientists could breathe. As Jim and his team dropped farther and farther, they watched the sunlight from the mine entrance fade from a pencil-thin beam to a pinpoint. Then, it faded to nothing.

In the dust and rubble of a tunnel, geologists David M'she (right) and Svetlana Kotelnikova examine a rock sample.

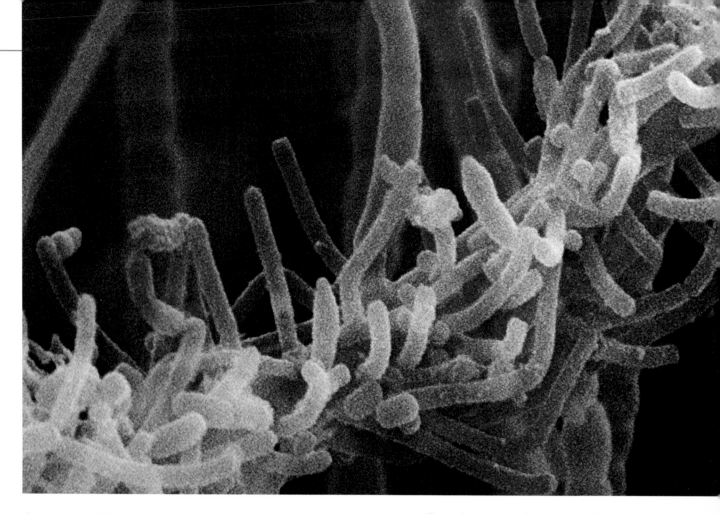

Strange Bacteria

"It's an eerie feeling, knowing you're that far down," says Jim. Not long ago, biologists thought it was impossible for life to exist deep beneath Earth's surface. They believed that every kind of life needs the same kind of materials, such as oxygen, that are abundant at Earth's surface. But discoveries by Jim and other researchers have challenged that idea.

These scientists study samples from deeply drilled wells. From the samples, the scientists have determined that there are bacteria living nearly two kilometers (about one mile) beneath the surface. Even stranger, some of the bacteria seem to live on little more than water, hydrogen, sulfur, and the minerals in rock.

These deep-living bacteria are sometimes called extremophiles, or lovers of extremes. Extremophiles are

These bacteria, shown magnified 500 times, live at hydrothermal vents on the ocean floor. Hydrothermal vents are cracks in the seafloor. The vents let extremely hot water carrying chemicals, such as hydrogen sulfide, and minerals come up into the ocean. The bacteria shown above are able to live in the hot water near the vents.

The Beginnings of Life

How might life have begun on Earth or on another planet? Scientists don't know. But by studying fossils, or remains of ancient plants and animals, and life on our planet today, they can make some guesses.

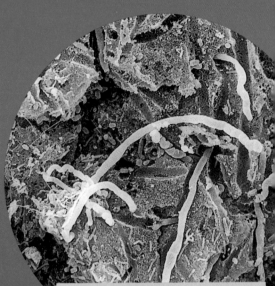

From the Skies

Comets and asteroids carry water and organic molecules from space. Life may have developed from these substances. Perhaps that is how organisms first formed on Earth.

Under the Sea

In 1977 scientists found another possible explanation for the beginnings of life. They found deep-sea bacteria, some of which are shown above magnified many times. These bacteria are able to live without oxygen. Life on Earth or another planet could have begun with microorganisms like these that live on sulfur and other chemicals.

In 1999 scientists found another type of bacteria that live in extreme conditions. Bacteria in Lake Vostok in Antarctica do not need light as a source of energy. This lake is frozen beneath almost 4 kilometers (about 2.5 miles) of ice. Light has not reached the lake for millions of years. If bacteria can live there, maybe they can live elsewhere under very extreme conditions.

Lightning Strikes

Food for Earth's first life forms could have also come from the air. In a 1953 experiment, University of Chicago scientists Stanley Miller and Harold Urey sent sparks through a container holding the gases methane, ammonia, water vapor, and hydrogen. These gases could have been in young Earth's atmosphere and could have been struck by lightning.

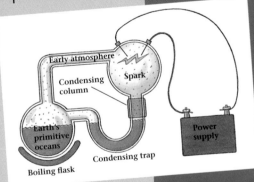

Early atmosphere
Condensing column
Spark
Earth's primitive oceans
Power supply
Condensing trap
Boiling flask

The experiment didn't include oxygen, because scientists don't think oxygen existed in the early atmosphere. After a week, the container held a yellow-brown "ocean." It included several types of amino acids, molecules that are the building blocks of proteins and the beginnings of life.

found in places where it was once thought to be impossible for anything to be living.

Extremophiles include bacteria that grow around cracks on the ocean floor. The bacteria live there even though superhot fluids pour out from the cracks. The water near the cracks can be hotter than 350° C (about 660° F). The weight of water above the ocean floor prevents the water from boiling. Although the water remains liquid, environments around cracks on the ocean floor are extreme.

Extremophiles also include bacteria living beneath frozen lakes in Antarctica where temperatures are -55.5°C (-68°F). Scientists like the team in South Africa study extremophiles to better understand how life can exist in extreme environments.

(below, top)
Scientists found this rock in the South African mine. The boxed part of the rock is called carbon leader. The scientists hope to find bacteria inside the carbon leader.

(below, bottom)
T. C. (left) and Duane Moser examine the wall of the mine. They are looking for a good place to get a sample.

As the scientists traveled down to the bottom of the South African mine, they felt the increased air pressure push on their eardrums. The air pressure at the bottom of this mine is twice that of air at the surface. The researchers stepped out of the elevator with their sampling equipment and began their journey through the mine. They were soon soaked in sweat. This terrible heat was something that Jim and the rest of the team, led by Princeton University geologist T. C. Onstott, had to live with for the day. Miners have to live with it every day.

The scientists had to walk very long distances in the heat and humidity to reach the freshly exposed rock surfaces at the ends of the tunnels. The tunnels were quite far from the lights in the main part of the mine. They were lit only by flashlights and by the lamps on the scientists' helmets.

On the surface the scientists have set up a rock laboratory. Jim (left) and Duane crush the carbon leader in an oxygen-free chamber to reach the untouched material inside.

Collecting Samples

But Jim, T. C., and the others weren't thinking about the heat or the dark. As they worked, questions raced through their minds. What organisms could live down here? Were there bacteria? How many were there? Could they bring the bacteria to the surface without harming or contaminating them?

The scientists took samples in areas where the gold miners had been working only a day or two before. They looked for blackened rock called carbon leader, where they thought they might find bacteria. Other scientists had previously found bacteria in carbon leader in South African mines. Gold miners also look for carbon leader because it contains gold and uranium.

The scientists used hammers to carefully chip out large pieces of carbon leader from the rock. They wore gloves to avoid contaminating the samples. Then, they put the pieces into clean bags.

Back at their makeshift laboratory on the surface, the scientists opened the bags. They used a glove box filled

Here researcher Mary de Flaun checks a sample to make sure it is not contaminated. To check it, she mixes a small piece of the sample with some chemicals. These chemicals bring out a red-purple dye that scientists sprayed on the rock layer while it was still in the mine. The dye reveals the degree of contamination.

Once the samples are ready, Jim (right) adds chemicals to the samples and watches to see what happens. T. C. looks on.

with nitrogen gas instead of oxygen. Nitrogen keeps alive the bacteria that would die in oxygen. Using the glove box, the scientists carefully removed the outer layers of each rock. Then, they crushed the inner part of the rock and put the pieces into test tubes. The test tubes held different kinds of food and chemicals. They observed the test tubes closely. Would the bacteria grow? If a test tube held the right mix of food and chemicals, it would turn cloudy as the bacteria in the rock multiplied. The scientists would then study the bacteria to find out how they live, what they need to live, and how they may be related to other bacteria.

The team expected to find some very unusual forms of life in the mine. But they were surprised when they found bacteria that lived on minerals in the rock and on a gas called methane. These bacteria used oxygen when it was present and switched to methane when it wasn't. Some were giants of the underground world. They measured 4 to 5 microns (0.00016 to 0.00020 inch) across. Most kinds of deep-rock bacteria are much smaller.

Most surprising to T. C. and the other scientists were the numbers and variety of bacteria they found. There were nearly 100 times more bacteria than scientists had seen in any other underground place. "It was a complete, total shock," T. C. says. There may be much more life underground than scientists previously believed.

The team doesn't know why there were such large numbers and so many different kinds of bacteria in the carbon leader. Scientists haven't yet found out how long the bacteria have lived there. Maybe bacteria in the South African mine have lived undisturbed for 2 billion years. Could this mean that there is life on Mars now, deep under the surface? Perhaps future research expeditions on Mars will answer this question.

Thermus is one kind of bacteria the scientists discovered in the South African mine. Living at 3.2 kilometers (about 2 miles) underground, it is one of the deepest-living land bacteria known. Studying extreme bacteria like *Thermus* might help scientists figure out whether life could exist on other planets.

6

SEARCHING FOR ET

"I decided long ago that this was the most important question I could try to answer."—Jill Tarter

Jill Tarter couldn't believe her eyes. The slanted line that appeared on her computer screen was exactly what she was looking for. It was a sign that her radio telescope had picked up a signal from outer space. In the past she was always quick to identify the source of the radio signals. Sometimes the signal was made by an orbiting satellite or a spacecraft. Often the radio signals came from a transmitter on the ground.

But this morning in 1997 was different. Every time she pointed the radio telescope in the direction of the star YZCETI, the signal appeared. When the telescope was pointed in another direction, the signal went away. Jill had been looking for years for something like this. Was it a message from an extraterrestrial civilization?

Jill is leading the largest search for extraterrestrial signals. Scientists in the search, called Project Phoenix, are examining 1,000 sunlike stars for signs of intelligent life. Jill is a radio astronomer, or an astronomer who uses radio telescopes. She inspired the idea for the character played by Jodie Foster in the movie *Contact*.

Jill's search has taken a lot of hard work. She's been looking for more than 30 years, but she still hasn't found a signal. "But I can't think of a more important question to work on," she says. "I decided long ago that this was the most important question I could try to answer."

(above)
Jill and other astronomers are trying to answer the question "Are we alone?" They do this by listening for radio signals that may be sent by other civilizations out in space.

(left)
From 1996 to 1998 the Project Phoenix astronomers watched for signals from this almost 43-meter (140-foot) diameter radio telescope at the National Radio Astronomy Observatory in Green Bank, West Virginia.

Since 1998 Project Phoenix has been located at the Arecibo Observatory in Puerto Rico, shown above. Project Phoenix uses the radio telescope at the observatory. In 1974 this telescope sent the most powerful broadcast ever purposely directed into space.

On the morning Jill saw the signal, she sent e-mail to other scientists at the SETI (Search for Extra Terrestrial Intelligence) Institute in Mountain View, California, to tell them she had found "something interesting." Then, she phoned her husband and told him not to expect her home for quite a while. Until she figured out where the signal was coming from, she wasn't leaving the Green Bank radio telescope in West Virginia. "I was supposed to leave for the airport that day. But I decided that I was going to stay. I wasn't going to leave when there might be a signal."

What Are the Chances?—Drake's Equation

What are the chances of detecting a signal from another civilization? That depends on several things, including how many other civilizations there are.

How can astronomers estimate the number of technological civilizations, or civilizations with advanced technology, in space? Astronomer Frank Drake came up with a formula to make an estimate when he was working as a radio astronomer at the National Radio Astronomy Observatory in Green Bank. He is now the president of the SETI Institute.

The formula is called Drake's Equation. Drake's Equation identifies factors that scientists need to know to determine the number of technological civilizations in the stars.

This is Drake's Equation:

$$N = R^* \times f_p \times n_e \times f_1 \times f_i \times f_c \times L$$

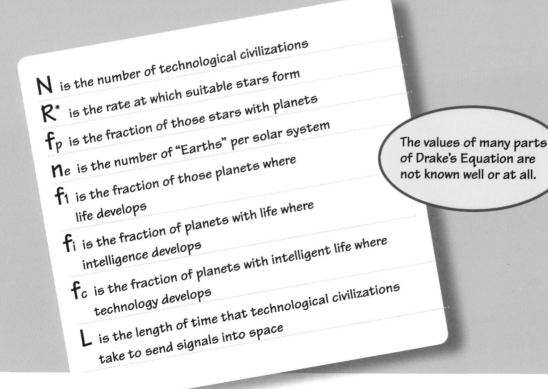

N is the number of technological civilizations

R^* is the rate at which suitable stars form

f_p is the fraction of those stars with planets

n_e is the number of "Earths" per solar system

f_1 is the fraction of those planets where life develops

f_i is the fraction of planets with life where intelligence develops

f_c is the fraction of planets with intelligent life where technology develops

L is the length of time that technological civilizations take to send signals into space

The values of many parts of Drake's Equation are not known well or at all.

SETI Institute astronomer Seth Shostak is hopeful that an alien signal will be detected. He thinks that improved technology might make this possible. "In two decades we'll have an experiment that's thousands of times better than what we now have."

Who's There?

The discovery of intelligent life elsewhere in the universe is the main goal of astrobiology. This discovery would prove that life can start on another planet and can develop intelligence. There are about 100 billion stars in our galaxy and billions of possible solar systems. So some astronomers believe that the existence of intelligent life elsewhere is not only likely, but almost certain. Contacting that life would change the way we see our place in the universe.

Before we start thinking about what to say to an extraterrestrial caller, astronomers need to detect the call's signal. To do that, they must come up with the right answers to two questions. First, where in the sky should they point their telescopes? And second, in what form should they expect a message from ET?

Astronomers believe the first signs from an extraterrestrial civilization are likely to come as light. This light could be visible, radio, ultraviolet, or X-rays. The nearest star is more than four light-years away. A light-year is the distance light travels in one year. Thus a radio signal would take four years to reach Earth from the nearest star. Forget flying saucers or spaceships.

Continuing to Search

The chance to be the first person to discover a signal from another intelligent civilization pulled SETI Institute astronomer Seth Shostak away from another career in research. He joined Project Phoenix to help make a discovery that he hopes will change our world. "It's a real team effort," he says.

Despite their optimism, the team members know that they may not see results in their lifetimes. "If you were to ask me if I think we're going to find ET today, I'd say the

Flashes of Light

The CfA's Oak Ridge Observatory is in Harvard, Massachusetts. There a team of scientists led by Paul Horowitz, a physicist at Harvard University, is investigating the possibility that an intelligent civilization could be directing powerful lasers toward Earth.

The team, working with astronomers from the CfA, is looking at 2,500 sunlike stars. They search in visible light, the kind of light we see with our eyes. For this search they use an optical telescope, a telescope made to focus and detect visible light. The team is searching for bright flashes of light that might be laser beams from outer space.

Paul Horowitz and his team look for laser pulses using the special detector shown beside Paul in the small photo. The detector attaches to the 1.5-meter (61-inch) diameter Wyeth reflector telescope, which is shown in the large photo.

chances aren't that high," says Seth. "But on the other hand, you're certainly not going to find anything just sitting here. You'll only find it at the telescope. That's the appeal. You don't really expect to find anything, but you could."

Most of the astronomers' work at the telescope is done with the help of a computer. The computer analyzes, or studies, the signals received from each star at which the telescope points. Something of possible interest is detected about once every ten minutes. But the computer usually decides that the signals aren't from outer space.

"Maybe a couple of times a day, we get a signal that is worthy of being drawn to the computer screen," says Seth. When that happens, the scientists look at the graph on the screen. The graph tells them the strength of the signal for each wavelength in the range the telescope detects. The brightness of the dots on the screen indicates signal strength.

If the screen shows a bright vertical line, the radio telescope is picking up signals from Earth, such as radio or television signals. The frequency of a radio signal from a station does not change with time. However, the frequency of a radio signal from a star changes slightly as Earth orbits the sun and rotates, or turns, on its axis. This change causes the line on the computer to "slant." A radio signal received from an artificial Earth satellite or spacecraft also changes in wavelength and will appear on the screen as a slanted line. The scientists only pay attention to the narrow lines on their computer screens because the signals they are looking for have only a narrow range of wavelengths.

To find out if the slanted line, like the one Jill found on her screen, is a signal from a spacecraft or a star, SETI astronomers use

This is a graph that Project Phoenix astronomers saw on their computer. The slanted line represents a signal detected by the radio telescope. Every second, new data points appear on the top line, the other points move down, and the oldest ones drop off the bottom.

Menu
The menu provides a choice of ways astronomers can view data.

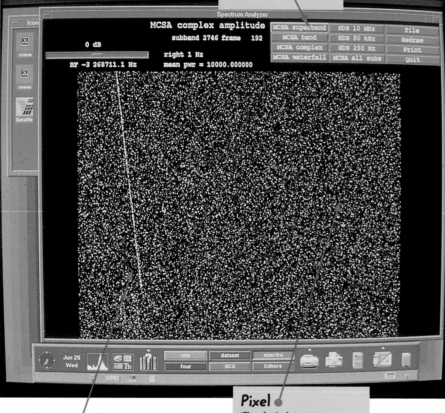

Signal
The slight slant represents a change in frequency over time, or the Doppler effect. It is caused by the source's motion in the direction the telescope is pointed.

Pixel
The brightness indicates signal strength. The dim signals appear as "static" and are not important.

a second radio telescope at another location. But on the morning of June 23, 1997, when Jill found the slanted line, she and John Dreher, another SETI Institute astronomer, couldn't use the second telescope. The telescope, which is located in England, had been struck by lightning the day before. The only thing Jill and John could do was to use their own radio telescope there in West Virginia.

They studied the unidentified signal for a few hours. Then, John began to sense something wasn't right. The star they had directed the telescope toward was setting in the west. But the change in the frequency of its radio signal appeared the way it would if the star were going the other way. Jill then looked at a table of characteristics of signals expected from satellites and found the answer. The signal had been sent from a satellite launched by NASA to study the sun.

Jill and other astronomers involved in Project Phoenix hope that they will one day turn their radio telescopes to just the right star and detect just the right signals. But even if intelligent beings aren't located soon, scientists are confident that they will eventually find some kind of extraterrestrial life.

"We happen to live in a very special point in time," says Jill. "For thousands of years, people have asked...'Is there intelligent life elsewhere in the universe?' Right now, for the first time, scientists and engineers can work to try to answer their question."

Astronomers have found planets orbiting other stars. They have found water and organic chemicals in space and amino acids in meteorites. And biologists have found life on Earth existing under conditions that are extreme compared to those we experience. Each discovery offers a clue in the search for life.

GLOSSARY

asteroids Rocklike materials that orbit the sun, mostly between Mars and Jupiter. Asteroids range in length from less than a meter (about three feet) to hundreds of kilometers (hundred of miles).

atmosphere Gases around a star or planet, such as Earth.

bacteria Single-celled organisms that often grow in large colonies, or groups.

carbon leader A thin layer of rock found in another rock. Carbon leader is mostly made of carbon, an important organic element. Since carbon is one of the basic things needed for life, scientists think carbon leader is a good place to search for life underground. They have already found bacteria in carbon leader.

carbon monoxide A molecule composed of one carbon atom and one oxygen atom. Carbon monoxide is found in car exhaust.

comet A chunk of frozen gases, water, dirt, and rock that orbits the sun. Comets are various sizes.

constellation A set of stars in the sky that forms a recognizable pattern in people's imaginations.

contamination The act of making something unclean.

detector A device that detects light coming from an object.

extraterrestrial Something beyond Earth.

extremophile An organism that thrives in extreme environments. Extremophiles are found in cracks in the ocean floor, beneath frozen lakes, and in other remote areas.

fossil The remains, such as the skeleton, of an ancient organism.

galaxy An extremely large collection of stars that can be seen in the sky as separate from other such collections. Our sun is in the Milky Way galaxy.

gas The state of matter in which molecules can be far apart from one another and move about independently. A gas has no definite shape. Gas spreads out to fill any container it is in. Other states of matter are solid and liquid. A solid has a definite shape, and a liquid takes the shape of its container, but may not fill it.

humidity The amount of moisture in the air.

life The quality that distinguishes living organisms. It includes many activities, such as digestion of food, growth, and reproduction.

light-year The distance that light travels in one year. One light-year is about $9\frac{1}{2}$ trillion kilometers (about 6 trillion miles).

meteorite A solid chunk of matter from space that has fallen to Earth.

model An explanation for an event based on observations of nature's behavior. Models are useful if they can accurately predict future events.

molecular cloud A large cloud made of about 99 percent gas and 1 percent dust. It is thought that new stars are made in such clouds.

molecule A collection of atoms that are bonded to one another and hard to separate.

optical telescope A telescope designed to focus and detect visible light.

organic molecule A molecule that contains carbon, an element essential to life on Earth.

planetary geologist A scientist who studies the material of which planets are made.

radio telescope An antenna, or "dish," that collects radio waves given off by objects in space.

radio waves Light that we cannot see with our eyes. In the wave model of light, radio waves have longer wavelengths than other forms of light.

satellite A natural or human-made object that moves in orbit around a planet.

space probe A spacecraft with instruments used to gather information about outer space. A space probe can travel far from Earth.

spectrograph An instrument used to separate light into a spectrum and record it. A spectrograph is often attached to a telescope.

spectrum For light visible to human eyes, a spectrum is the set of colors, from red to violet, that we see. For example, the rainbow formed when sunlight passes through a prism represents a spectrum.

stellar speedometer A device that measures the speed of stars as they move in a direction toward or away from Earth.

visible light Light that we can see with our eyes.

water vapor Water that is in a gaseous state.

Further Reading

Angelo, Joseph A. *The Extraterrestrial Encyclopedia: Our Search for Life in Outer Space.* New York, NY: Facts on File, 1991.

Couper, Heather, and Nigel Henbest. *Is Anybody Out There?* New York, NY: Dorling Kindersley Publishing, 1998.

Desonie, Dana. *Cosmic Collisions.* New York, NY: Henry Holt, 1996.

Digregorio, Barry E., Gilbert V. Levin, and Patricia Ann Straat. *Mars: The Living Planet.* Berkeley, CA: Frog Limited, 1997.

Fradin, Dennis Brindell. *Is There Life on Mars?* New York, NY: Simon & Schuster, 1999.

Miles, Lisa, and Alistair Smith. *The Usborne Complete Book of Astronomy and Space.* Tulsa, OK: EDC Publications, 1998.

Scott, Elaine. *Close Encounters: Exploring the Universe with the Hubble Space Telescope.* New York, NY: Hyperion Books for Children, 1998.

Skurzynski, Gloria. *Discover Mars.* Washington, D.C.: National Geographic Society, 1998.

Wunsch, Susi Trautmann. *The Adventures of Sojourner: The Mission to Mars That Thrilled the World.* New York, NY: Mikaya Press, 1998.

INDEX

Acknowledgments

Many people made this book possible, including the scientists featured in the preceding pages who took time away from their important research projects to be interviewed and to review the manuscript. But special thanks should go to Audrey Bryant and Erica Thrall of Turnstone Publishing for making this book what it is; to Ralph Harvey, my tent mate in Antarctica, and the National Science Foundation, for allowing me to pluck off the ice sheet pieces of the primordial solar system no one else has seen; to Charlie Telesco, Scott Fisher, and Ray Jayawardhana for showing me at the Cerro Tololo Inter-American Observatory in Chile what planet hunting is all about; and last, but not least, to my wife, Kathy, who entertained our daughter, Rachel, while I rushed to finish the manuscript for this book.

Credits

Photographs courtesy of:

Brenner, Dave/University of Alaska Sea Grant: 7; CfA: 19; Charbonneau, Dave: 20; Chase, Jon: 26 middle, 26 right; Corbis: 5; Dame, Tom/CfA: 22, 23, 24, 25, 26–27 bottom, 26 left; Dover Publications, Inc.1992: 6; Fletcher, Bill and Sally: 27 top, 46 top left; Frazietz, C-K: 39; Gubb, Louise/SABA: 42, 44, 47, 48, 49, 50; Horowitz, Paul: 57; JPL: cover background, 1 background, 3 top, 8 left, 9 main image; Latham, David/CfA: 12, 16; Mayor, Michel: 18; McCarthy, Mike: 2 left, 28, 29; McDonald, Kim: 2 right, 30, 31, 32, 33, 35, 36; Moser, Duane/Princeton University: 47 top; Murray, Jack: 17; NASA: 2 middle, 3 bottom, 9 inset, 10–11, 37, 38, 40–41; The Robotics Institute, Carnegie Mellon: 1 inset, 34; STSCI, Hubble Heritage: 8 top; Shostak, Seth/SETI: 52, 53, 54, 55, 56, 58, 59; Southam, Gordon/Northern Arizona University: 51; Stefanik, Robert/Oak Ridge Observatory: 17; Walker, Sean: 4, 13, 15; Wirsen, Carl/WHOI: 45, 46 right.

The illustration on page 21 is by Lynette Cook. The illustration on page 46 bottom is by David Griffin. The illustration on page 43 is by Jill Leichter.